HALIMA

ENLIGHTENED PASSION

By Firew Bekele

HALIMA

ENLIGHTENED PASSION

Edited By Firew Bekele

August, 2021

Table of Contents

Contents

1. INDIAN OCEAN SLAVE TRADE 4

2. FREED AFRICAN SLAVE GIRLS AND MISSIONARIES IN EGYPT 9

3. MEMORIES OF HOME COUNTRY AND CAPTURE 16

4. RELEASE AND MANUMISSION 26

5. EDUCATION AND IMPROVEMENT 41

6. HALIMA: A MODEL LIFE 52

References 62

1. INDIAN OCEAN SLAVE TRADE

The Indian Ocean slave trade was multi-directional and changed over time. To meet the demand for menial labor, slaves sold to Muslim slave merchants by local slave raiders, Ethiopian chiefs and kings from the interior, were sold over the centuries to customers in Egypt, the Arabian peninsula, the Persian Gulf, India, the Far East, the Indian Ocean islands, Somalia and Ethiopia.

During the second half of the 19th century and early 20th century, slaves shipped from Ethiopia had a high demand in the markets of the Arabian peninsula and elsewhere in the Middle East. They were mostly domestic servants, though some served as agricultural laborers, or as water carriers, herdsmen, seamen, camel drivers, porters, washerwomen, masons, shop assistants and cooks. The most fortunate of the men worked as the officials or bodyguards of the ruler and emirs, or as business managers for rich merchants. They enjoyed significant personal freedom and occasionally held slaves of their own. Besides Javanese and Chinese girls brought in from the Far East, young Ethiopian females were among the most valued concubines. The most beautiful ones often enjoyed a wealthy lifestyle, and became mistresses of the elite or even mothers to rulers. The principal sources of these slaves, all of whom passed through Matamma, Massawa and Tadjoura on the

Red Sea, were the southwestern parts of Ethiopia, in the Oromo and Sidama country.

The most important outlet for Ethiopian slaves was undoubtedly Massawa. Trade routes from Gondar, located in the Ethiopian Highlands led to Massawa via Adwa. Slave drivers from Gondar took 100-200 slaves in a single trip to Massawa, the majority of who were female.

A small number of eunuchs were also acquired by the slave merchants in the southern parts of Ethiopia. Mainly consisting of young children, they led the most privileged lives and commanded the highest prices in the Islamic global markets because of their rarity. They served in the harems of the affluent or guarded holy sites. Some of the young boys had become eunuchs due to the battle traditions that were at the time endemic to Arsi and Borena of southern Ethiopia. However, the majority came from the Badi Folia principality in the Jimma region, situated to the southeast of Enarea. The local Oromo rulers were so disturbed by the custom that they had driven out all of those in their kingdoms who practiced it.

Even as Europeans carved out enclaves on the coast of India, the sidis of Janjira continued to wield power and other Africans continued to arrive as slaves in India. Perhaps the most renowned of these was Malik Ambar, an enslaved Ethiopian who became the effective ruler of the inland kingdom of Ahmadnagar from 1602 to 1626. Malik Ambar made an alliance with the sidis of Janjira. Together, the sidis and Malik Ambar stood against the Mughal Empire. Malik Ambar also employed sidis on his vessels. A list of ship masters who received maritime passes from the Portuguese in 1618-1622 included a number of sidis, all under the employ of the king of Ahmadnagar. In addition Malik Seto, an Ethiopian-born seafarer, commanded a large ship that sailed between western India and Arabia in 1616; among the men under his command was a European.

2. FREED AFRICAN SLAVE GIRLS AND MISSIONARIES IN EGYPT

In early March 1887 a dozen of freed slave girls arrived at the Ezbekieh Boarding School run by American Presbyterian missionaries with fifty pounds and forty yards of calico for dresses. They had been sent by Sir Evelyn Baring (Lord Cromer), the British agent and consul general in Egypt from 1883 to 1907, from the Cairo Home for Freed Female Slaves, where they had been temporarily lodged. The dozen girls had been intercepted by British boats on the Red Sea or Egyptian police in caravans coming over land into Egypt ten years after the slave trade had been officially banned into and through the country and a few years before slavery itself became illegal. Their paths into slavery varied; their path out brought the hundreds young girls together.

Picture: African Arab Slave Trade, 1884, Library of Congress / Science Photo Library

The enslaved in Egypt and the Islamic Middle East were mostly illiterate and left few memoirs. The lack of slave narratives and "silence of slaves" have led to an absence of voices, faces, and names of slaves from historical accounts. Scholars have recently begun to rectify this omission over innovative methodologies and literary strategies. Ehud Toledano argues, "by exploring the available options, the dilemma at hand, and the choice made by the enslaved, we can see agency and resistance emerge out of misery and powerlessness," as he focuses on the relationship that bound the enslaved and slavers. Eve Troutt Powell analyzes memoirs that have come to light, critically reading texts and raising issues about voice and memory. The examination for new sources - visual and literary - continues alongside efforts to push theoretical understandings of slavery in the Middle East.

American missionaries were prodigious

writers who kept careful records. Through years of study and practice, they mastered Arabic, and their long residences in the field for decades running a network of educational, medical, and welfare institutions gave them impressive knowledge of their host country. They also came with their own religious and racial baggage, which must be carefully unpacked when investigating the records they left of encounters with freed slaves. These records can be read critically to get at the lives and choices of the dozen African girls who landed on their doorsteps. The story of these girls provides a look at the paths into and out of slavery, drawing attention to the youth of most of those caught in the net of the slave merchants and destined for service in the Ottoman Empire.

Academics have debated the demise of slavery in Egypt and the fate of freed slaves. The question of the demise of slavery, and whether it ended with a whimper or a bang from internal or external pressures, is tied to views of the importance of slavery in Egyptian society. Gabriel Baer tends to discredit the efficacy of bans on the slave trade enacted from the 1850s by Ottoman-Egyptian governors and credits the British for effectively ending the trade; he finds that the presence of guilds and absence of a free labor market hindered the absorption of freed slaves into the Egyptian society and economy. Judith Tucker sees slavery fading out more naturally. *"Never of signal importance in the country, the institution gradually crumbled,"* as over the course of the century the significance of female slaves, who were the majority, became *"ever more symbolic"*. Slavery *"swiftly became an anachronism"* and was abolished with ease. "Once the supply was cut off, and slaves could seek manumission freely, the institution in Egypt died a painless death." Tucker claims that manumitted slave women were easily assimilated "into the very classes that had formerly possessed them," with race and an earlier slave status holding no stigma.

Other scholars occupy a middle ground. Liat Kozma, focusing on legal and police records, has sketched the abolition of the slave trade through numerous bans "as a long process of readjustment" in which the Ottoman-Egyptian legal system moved from the Islamic sanction of slavery to the *"suppression of the slave trade as unjust and inhumane."* *In the process, "slaves came to be seen more as persons and less as property."* Powell, looking at literary accounts and the press, sees slavery as of signal importance in Egypt's complicated colonial relationship to the Sudan. She notes the difficulty of letting go of an institution that was central to conceptions of family and intimacy, and her examination of a renowned slave trading trial in 1894, which implicated leading notables, highlights this. For Toledano, Powell, and Kozma, race mattered, and freed slaves, most of whom were of African origins, struggled with marginality, vulnerability, and limited choices.

3. MEMORIES OF HOME COUNTRY AND CAPTURE

In the period in which the American Presbyterian missionaries established a network of institutions in Egypt, the slave trade spiked, predominantly during the cotton boom of the 1860s, when Egyptian cotton replaced the American commodity on the market. Slaves were brought in as a result of the wealth flooding the country from cotton profits as well as for agricultural slavery in the south. Most were domestic slaves (concubines and/or servants) in a system that did not reproduce itself and thus needed a constant influx of new slaves. The girls who landed in the Ezbekiah Boarding School ranged in age from eight to fourteen, consistent with Reda Mowafi's observation that the largest proportion of slaves imported into Egypt were under fifteen. Merchants preferred younger slaves because they fetched a higher price, needed less food, and were less likely to resist during their transport. Those eleven to fourteen or fifteen were the most expensive, primarily because at that age they were young enough to be trained within a family to be a good servant but old enough to start working and participate in sexual activity, even if unwanted. In any case, the girls taken in by the missionaries were definitely old enough to have memories of family and home.

The roots of the a dozen of were never precisely chronicled. A British slave trade abolitionist who visited them in the school and heard them sing some hymns "in their own language" claimed the girls came from "Oromo country." But Anna Thompson, an American Presbyterian missionary who worked in Egypt from 1872 to 1932, noted a few years after the girls had come to the school, "there were Nubians among them, Sudanese and Ethiopians." Later, in an anonymous pamphlet on one of the freed slaves produced in the 1930s or so, they are listed as seven Ethiopians and five Sudanese; Oromos became Ethiopians, and the Nubians were folded into the Sudanese. The native tongues that they claimed, and the language in which they spoke to one another are not clear. One of the girls, named Susan, was from Nubia, according to Thompson:

In her inimitable way, after some weeks, she told how she had been carried away with her family and villagers by the Mahdi and his troops, and how she used to play with the Mahdi's children…. Her singing about the Mahdi and the white "hat owners" (English troops) as she learned it at Khartoum, was always listened to with pleasure and sadness, and she and two others could dance in the very peculiar Sudanese style.

Susan had clear memories of home that came through in her singing and dancing, though the latter was suppressed as she became socialized into proper Christian behavior at the boarding school. The missionary teacher, Adela Brown, reflected on the summer of 1890 when Susan and one or two of the other girls stayed at the school in Cairo, unable to go home to relatives as the Egyptian girls had. Missionaries and government officials made no attempt to return these girls to their native villages, but their longing was apparent. "I heard from them many interesting items about their native land. It was their delight to talk about their parents and home and country. They seemed to have vivid pictures in their minds, but whether they were fancy or real I cannot say." The girls had strong memories of home that they liked to relate, and they listened to one another.

By distinction, another girl, Halima, seemed to remember little, though she was thought to be about eleven years old when she arrived at the boarding school. "Years later when questioned by friends, she could tell little of her early life," recorded her pamphleteer. She may have recalled little or may have found the memories too painful and chose to bury them deep inside. She did remember her village home in the mountains of Ethiopia in the western part of the country; the village name; and a war, in the midst of which she and some other girls were snatched while at play near the village. She did not know by what route she had been brought to Egypt, so the pamphleteer had her brought her up the Nile on a boat, rescued, and put on a train for Cairo. The "Oromo girls" had been intercepted by a British ship on the Red Sea – thus earning the name "Red Sea waifs" – and disembarked at Port Suez, where they were transferred to Cairo. Some of these girls ended up at the Ezbekiah boarding school. Halima was a child when she was taken from her family and shipped to Egypt. The pain of that separation stayed with her, as Halima related, "I cried for my mother whenever I was awake, for a year."

Susan seems to have been displaced twice, once with her family from Nubia to Khartoum and once on her own.

She remembered being at play with another child, "getting gum from a tree," when a man on horseback carried her off. She was then passed from one person to another until she was captured by the police in Egypt.

Picture: <u>Ethiopian Slave-girl. Egypt, Engraving 1879. (Photo by: Universal History Archive/Universal Images Group via Getty Images)</u>

Her itinerary into Egypt could have been a desert caravan led by Bedouins, who smuggled slaves to Asyut to avert bans on the slave trade. The Egyptian police force had turned from protecting owners' property rights and returning runaway slaves to enforcing the bans on the slave trade, mirroring a shift in the Ottoman Empire, where government officials had come to side with the enslaved more than the enslavers.

The girls' memories of their homes and families come through the filter of missionary writings. At times the girls seemed eager to speak to Americans about their pasts; at other times they withheld their stories and sought to repress painful memories. The missionaries passed on only treats, weaning out pieces of the story and dismissing parts as childish fantasies.

Both the slave merchants and missionaries sought to redefine the religious identities of the girls. The missionaries claimed that the girls were given "Mohammedan names" by the slave merchants. By making this claim, the missionaries pointed to the recent and coercive nature of their conversion to Islam. At some point during the transport of their human cargo, slavers converted the enslaved to Islam in preparation for their sale in Egypt and often gave them new names to signal their new religious identity. By Islamic law, the enslaved were meant to be non-Muslims captured in war, but most were captured in raids, not war, and some were already Muslims. The missionaries allowed them to keep their names, whether given by parents or slavers, except in cases of repetition. The smaller of the two Mariseela's became Seela; and the smaller of the two Taroonga's became Susan, to evoke Aswan. Those named (like Susan and Halima) have only first names; there are no second or father's names. The erasure of family ties transforms the girls into orphans, which is how they are labeled and treated. Few of the other freed slave girls were named at all, and not naming is also significant. They were blank slates, ready for redemption in life or death.

4. RELEASE AND MANUMISSION

Missionaries, British abolitionists, colonial officers, Egyptian government officials, slave merchants, and the enslaved were all caught up in a contentious battle over slavery. The lines in this battle were not clearly drawn. Egyptians had mixed outlooks on slavery: those against the practice realized that stripping the Sudan of her population undermined Egyptian colonial ambitions and civilizing mission, that the slave trade as currently practiced contravened Islamic law, and that wage labor ultimately made more economic sense than slavery. But others profited from the trade, considered the slaves they owned assets that enhanced their prestige, saw slavery itself as civilizing and sanctioned by Islam, and could conceive of no alternative for local service. Sa`id, governor of Egypt (1854-1863), had banned the slave trade in 1854; but in the nonappearance of instruments to enforce it, the ban had been generally ineffective in stopping the slave trade though it began to change the way the legal system conceptualized slaves.

With the end of slavery in America,

British abolitionists turned their attention to slave practices in the Ottoman Empire and pushed for stricter treaties. The Anglo-Egyptian convention of 1877 outlawed the import and export of Ethiopian and Sudanese slaves, setting up four manumission bureaus throughout Egypt to supply documents as well as find work for freed slaves and schools for freed children. Banning the slave trade when owning slaves was still legal proved difficult to enforce, especially when merchants frequently passed off slaves as family members or as servants. The British, who used anti-slavery sentiments in England to mobilize support for their occupation of Egypt in 1882 and continued colonial presence, were afraid to tackle Islamic law and practices head on and moved slowly in outlawing slavery itself.

The outlawing of the slave trade when the demand for domestic slaves remained made life for smuggled slaves more precarious, as merchants took detours and risks to avert the watchful eyes of agents. Officials plugged one hole only to find slaves brought into Egypt through another route. One such avenue was the importation of slaves by pilgrims returning from Mecca. It was a tempting and lucrative trade, with a high mark-up: in the mid-1880s female slaves could be purchased in Mecca for about four pounds and sold in Egypt for thirty.

Officials sought to stop the smuggling of slaves by returning pilgrims after the prohibition of sale of slaves from family to family had gone into effect. Lieutenant-Colonel Schaefer, Director of the Slave Department, sent instructions to the commander at Port Suez in 1886. All pilgrims arriving at Suez, where most either disembarked from vessels or continued through the canal, were to be checked. Newly-brought slaves without manumission papers were to be taken from their masters and sent to the Cairo Home for Freed Women Slaves established the previous year; newly-brought slaves with manumission papers were to be given a choice whether they wanted to stay with their masters or not (some may have been married to their masters.) *If they are under 14 years,* he instructed, *it is better to send them to Cairo.* The guidelines for pilgrims traveling by ship were slightly different: "If bought recently and not over 12 years of age, they are to be brought on shore and sent to Cairo." Schaefer also instructed the commander at Suez to keep a record of "all negresses or Ethiopians were coming in," showing their names, masters if recently purchased or simply traveling, and what was done with them. Schaefer wrote Baring, "*I can assure you that not a single colored person has been allowed to be passed without our getting satisfactory explanations about her position.*" He writes her position by acknowledging that most of the "black or Ethiopian, male and female" who came before government officials were girls or women. Some 119 persons were checked at the police office, and forty-one were found to have been purchased in Jidda. Five or perhaps seven had no manumission papers and were taken from their masters and sent to the Home for Freed Slaves in Cairo. Those sent to the Home included a Halima, who was owned by Mustapha al-Minyawr, and a Trongue, owned by Sitt Agouche, showing both male and female ownership. Both Halima and Trongue were listed as Sudanese but no ages were given. These girls may have been those of the same name who later landed in the missionary school, though there is some discrepancy on origin, since the Halima previously mentioned was Ethiopian.

By whatever route they had come into Egypt, both the Halima and Susan who were later raised and schooled by the missionaries had first been sent to the

Home for Freed Women Slaves in Cairo. That home had been opened in January 1885 as the product of a joint effort by a committee in London associated with the British and Foreign Anti-Slavery Society (BFASS), which raised funds through subscriptions for the refuge, and a second committee in Cairo, presided over by Baring, which dealt with the logistics. Abolitionists argued that freed male slaves could find ready employment (indeed many ended up in the army) but that freed female slaves would turn to a life of vice and prostitution to survive. This assumption stemmed from a belief that Africans were prone to sexual excess and crime unless properly supervised. The lack of such a home was thought to have impeded the emancipation of slaves and enforcement of the convention of 1877. Toward that end, Sarah Amos, a feminist, activist, and abolitionist, was one of the main advocates and organizers of the Home, getting it started in the neighborhood of Faggala and setting up Mrs. Crewe, an Englishwoman who spoke fluent Arabic, as matron. Crewe's fluency in Arabic would have helped in communication with those slaves who had been resident in Egypt for some time but not the newly enslaved, fresh from Africa.

The Home for Freed Slaves in Cairo acted as a refuge, staging area, and referral agency, and was part of Baring's agenda to turn freed slaves into a pool of waged female laborers or domestic servants. The newly freed slaves first had to be outfitted. Accompanied by a veteran from the Home, they purchased materials in town and returned to the home for sewing instruction, "for strange as it may seem, many of the black girls absolutely do not know how to use a needle," reported the secretary to the Cairo Committee for the Freed Slaves' Home. In this way, in 1886 alone over 600 dresses plus other garments were cut. Once outfitted, many of the freed slaves did not stay long. Mrs. Crewe helped place them in homes as domestic servants, and they were quickly snatched up, for demand for such servants exceeded supply. Initial reports suggest that the freed slaves were placed with Christian Syrians and Copts, but subsequent ones show that most were placed "in English families, others in French or Italian, and a few in native families of well-known respectability." Turn-around time was sometimes as fast as a few days. In short, the English were eager to turn slaves into paid domestic servants and became the first beneficiaries of this policy.

When Colonel Scott-Moncrieff, son-in-law of the chairman of the BFASS and a Cairo committee member, visited the Home in October 1885, he found that three of the nine or ten inhabitants of the home were children. Mrs. Crewe, who lived in the Home with her husband and children, claimed she could easily get these girls employment but preferred to train them herself to be good servants. The following year, sixteen Ethiopian girls – "all young, and some quite little girls," entered the home together, having been intercepted from pilgrims returning from

Mecca. None of the girls spoke Arabic, which was taken as a sign that they had been recently and illegally enslaved.

According to E. Crewe, the children had been transported by two slave merchants: six girls (and one boy) by Ali Pasha Wahba and ten girls (one boy, and two eunuchs) by the head of the Egyptian pilgrim caravan. In the subsequent six months, two of the new sixteen children were "sent out to service," one was married, and thirteen remained at the Home. Of those thirteen, the seven youngest went to Miss Whateley's Mission School, which had been set up by the British missionary for poor children. The annual report for the Home for 1886 noted that nearly all the Ethiopian girls were "in service, some of them earning over L 1 per month." Six of the youngest had learned to read Arabic, and it was hoped that some might become monitors or teachers in Miss Whately's School.

The youngest of these children, along with others, were included in the total number of children in the Home for 1886: "There are at present about a dozen of young children, from five to a dozen of years of age, in the HOME, some of whom have been rescued from Slave-dealers who were bringing them to Cairo to sell as Slaves." These girls received domestic training, in a set regime of household work, sewing, and ironing, "until such a time as they can earn their own livelihood." These a dozen of were sent to the American missionary boarding school in Cairo. They may have been sent when space became an issue: 225 slaves passed through the home in

1886, with 215 being placed in homes, and an average of fifteen to twenty occupants at any one time. The Home for Freed Women Slaves in Cairo was simply not equipped to care for young girls on a long-term basis; they would have taken up room and cost money to feed, house, and educate. The home was run on a relatively small budget, with some suggesting that it support itself, leading to a plan to utilize the labor of its inmates in laundry work. The small-scale operation was only marginally profitable, and the young girls could not contribute meaningfully to this plan or to their upkeep.

Halima, Susan, and the others may have been sent away for another reason as well. According to the Convention of

1877, freed slave children were to be educated, and the youngest had gone to Miss Whately's School. But the close association of girls in the Home with the missionary enterprise might have posed problems for Baring, who served as both president of the Home and British consul-general. The Home had to refrain from proselytizing among those who sought shelter, a condition the Cairo committee imposed on the project in order to make it acceptable to the Egyptian government, which gave the Home a 250 pound subvention. The question of slavery was controversial enough without adding religious conversion into the mix. Sending the girls to another location removed responsibility from the Home.

5. EDUCATION AND IMPROVEMENT

American missionaries who arrived in Egypt in the 1850s targeted Cairo and Asyut, a town in Upper Egypt with a large Coptic population thought to be receptive to Protestantism. Asyut was also a major depot in the slave trade and the destination for caravans on the "forty days road" (*darb al-arba`in*) from Darfur. By coincidence, the American Mission School was situated close to the spot where the slave caravans to Asyut came to rest.[32] Most American missionaries in Egypt came from northern states such as Pennsylvania, Ohio, and Illinois. They had seen battles over slavery split their country and church, giving rise to the United Presbyterian Church of North America

(UPCNA), founded in 1858. The UPCNA had a strong abolitionist platform and opened "freedmen's missions" after the American Civil War. But Americans in Egypt were there to save Egyptian souls, not to free African slaves, and treaded cautiously. Still, when opportunities presented themselves, they intervened, pressuring Copts to free their own slaves, alerting consuls to slave caravans, and giving refuge to rescued slaves. The missionaries benefited from their interventions. The first Muslim convert was an unnamed freed slave who joined the church in 1866, and twenty-two of the thirty-nine Muslims who had been baptized by 1883 were freed slaves. This is not surprising, notes Heather Sharkey, for *"In many ways, ex-slaves, like orphans, were perfect candidates for conversion, since by definition they lacked families who were apt to drag them back to the Muslim community under threats of death"*. And disinheritance was not a disincentive either, as they had little property to lose.

Missionary schools had also given shelter to freed slaves before. The Pressly Memorial Institute in Asyut had taken in three Sudanese girls from Darfur – Keltuma, Assa, and Fanna – who had been "rescued by the pluck of some Sudanese boys," according to Margaret McKown, founder of the school. The girls were placed in the boarding school, which gathered girls from area villages to train them in "common school education" and domestic work, and sent them back to their villages to minister to their own communities. At the school, the freed slaves received "the same training as the Egyptian girls" and were baptized three years after their arrival. But mobility for these freed African slave girls was more limited than those for Egyptian students. While the latter became teachers and Bible women, Keltuma and Assa (Fanna died prematurely) became matrons in the school and could be seen in a staff photograph taken in 1890. And although graduates of the school married Egyptian pastors, evangelicals, and teachers, the freed slaves joined a sisterhood of single women.

When Baring approached American missionaries in Cairo to take in the a dozen of little black girls and train them as they wished, the women missionaries saw an opportunity. "Knowing their need of instruction, and hoping that someday teachers might be educated from their number for central Africa or the far `upper country,' our mission consented," wrote Thompson. Evangelicals loathed the alternative: *"For want of funds these girls would have been given over to the Roman Catholics, had not the Protestant missionaries consented to take them,"* reported *The Christian,* a British periodical. The readers of *The Christian* were asked to send in shoes and simple dresses to be forwarded to the freed slaves.

The a dozen of girls who moved from the Home for Freed Slaves in Faggala to the boarding school in Ezbekiah in March 1887 had not been consulted about their change of home and school. When they arrived at their new abode, they did not take kindly to the new routine and structure. As Thompson explained in her annual report, "Some had been in the home [for Freed Women Slaves] for several months. These came to us much prejudiced against me. Strange stories had been told them of how we would make them work, abuse them, and make them Christians." In short, the girls had already developed their own information networks, most likely among the older freed slaves, and did not go quietly. In a letter to the *Women's Missionary Magazine*, Thompson elaborated on the girls' resistance: *"without any knowledge of what their parents' religion was, they were all zealous for the Moslem faith, and the older ones were for a time refractory, because they heard we were going to baptize them.*" Having been converted by slavers or illegally enslaved as Muslims, the girls were old enough to have a sense of their own religious identities. And having been through much forced change already, they initially resisted another change.

SLAVE BOATS ON THE NILE.

The missionaries maintained that they did not use compulsion to convert but hoped that once surrounded by Christian teaching and practice, the

African girls would prove receptive to the message. Their schooling included Arabic, English, Bible, catechism, housekeeping, and sewing, and some of their names are recorded in Thompson's class lists. By May, Thompson reported a *"kindly spirit … toward the Christian religion"*. The school cook, an unnamed freed Sudanese slave, played a key role in this transition, and started prayer meetings for the girls that summer. Within two years, one had been baptized and received into the church; two others were requesting baptism. One of those was Susan, who stood out as the most eager to learn about Christianity: "she prayed very earnestly that she and her companions might be used to carry the Gospel light to their people," wrote her teacher Adela Brown. Perhaps the girls thought Christian missionary work would be a way to get back home. Brown, who had a hard time seeing beyond color, reported that Susan was ahead of her class in Bible and catechism. "Her bright, sparkling eyes made her attractive (though she was very black), and her diligence and ambition cheered the heart of her teacher." In the fall of 1890, however, Susan grew ill, and in April 1891, four years after she had entered the school, she was taken to the hospital. Until then, the missionaries had delayed her baptism; but when she asked again to be baptized, one of the missionaries spoke to her about it. *"She passed away that night and was brought to the church the next day in her coffin. A few of us followed her to her resting place."* The missionaries took her lack of fear in the face of death to be a sign of Christian faith and victory, a soul saved, not a life lost.

Mortality among the a dozen of freed slave girls at the Ezbekiah School was high. One had arrived ill and died shortly thereafter; three others subsequently passed away, two of whom, according to Henrietta Harvey, had "given their hearts to Jesus and died trusting in him alone." Henrietta's husband, Dr. Harvey, had overseen the baptism of those girls, recording it in his diary. Henrietta admitted that the missionaries used to think slave mortality was high due to improper care, but experience showed that freed blacks also suffered from high rates of consumption. Arduous treks at young ages across deserts or by sea inflicted injuries and illnesses on the girls that shortened their lives. Even as Henrietta wrote, one girl was ill in her home. In spite of the loss of life, the missionaries took the conversions of the freed slave girls as a sign of their success.

Five years after Baring had sent a dozen of girls to the missionaries, only eight remained alive: one was ill; one was helping in a school in Asyut; one was a Bible woman under Anna Thompson's supervision; one who had been a servant was now in school at her own expense; one was set to go to Aden to teach freed slave girls in the Scotch Free Church mission with another Ethiopian (a plan that was delayed due to scurvy and fever in that mission); and three were servants in missionary families. One of the remaining eight later became matron of the Ezbekiah Boarding School under Ella Kyle.

6. HALIMA: A MODEL LIFE

Of the original a dozen of girls, American Presbyterian missionaries chose to highlight Halima's life story, memorializing her in a pamphlet. For them, her life was exemplary, in part because it remained inter- twined with the lives of the missionaries who had raised her and their descendants. American missionaries in Egypt were a tight knit group who, having left most of their kin in the USA, reconstituted themselves as a family. Sometimes they were interrelated, as offspring returned to the field after schooling to take up posts, and intermarriages between missionary families created second and third generations in the field. The missionaries appended the freed African slave girls to their families, or collective family, in roles familiar for African Americans in the USA: as servants, housekeepers, and nannies.

When Halima finished her schooling, she went with a missionary family to Asyut, where she took care of the home and children. She subsequently worked in other American and Egyptian homes, and *"became a general favorite and was known in the mission community from Khartoum to Alexandria."* Her pamphleteer tells us, she had "the pride and dignity of her race" and performed her service with "grace." In short, she served the church community well and was well-liked,

"Friendly and cheerful in disposition, she always rejoined to meet old friends or to make new ones."

Her life took a turn at about the age of twenty-five or so when she was called into a new sort of service.

In 1904, the American Mission in Egypt opened a hospital for women and children in Tanta, the fourth largest town in Egypt. Located in the Delta, Tanta was known for its *mawlid*, an annual celebration of the birth of a saint that drew thou- sands of visitors annually and prior to abolition had included a brisk market for slaves.

Halima and four of the other freed slave girls arrived in Tanta in response to a call from Lulu Harvey, daughter of Henrietta and Dr. Harvey. Lulu had become superintendent of nurses at the new hospital, but could not find native nurses. She turned to "the black girls whom she had known ever since their arrival in Cairo" to train them as assistants.

Lulu used a strategy similar to the one deployed by Clot Bey, the French medical expert hired by Mehmet Ali to modernize the practice of medicine in Egypt seventy years earlier. When Clot Bey opened the School for Midwives, his first recruits were slaves, followed by orphans and daughters of deceased military men, in short, girls who had no family on hand to veto this line of work. Likewise, Lulu turned to freed slave girls - now women - as recruits for her first class of nursing trainees. Although Egyptian women trained in the School for Midwives and worked as health care practitioners, few indigenous women worked in hospitals as nurses; it was not considered a suitable profession due to the gender mixing in a hospital.

Lulu Harvey trained Halima and the others, who came to Tanta with literacy in English and Arabic and the experience of having served in missionary institutions and American homes. Importantly for service in a missionary hospital, which coupled the provision of health care with proselytizing, Halima was also a Christian. *"To the Christians she was a sister in Christ – one whose faith gave one courage. To Mohammedans she was a bright example of Christian courtesy and kindness."* Halima joined the local Evangelical Church, where she was a regular attendee, and was considered a *"born nurse."* When the American hospital in Tanta was closed at the outbreak of World War I,

Halima found employment in the English mission hospital in Cairo. She then entered the School for Midwives (at about the age of forty), earning her certificate and taking up a job in a government hospital. Upon the reopening of the American hospital in Tanta in 1919, at which time it was expanded into a general hospital, she returned. There she served private patients, including ill American missionaries. The latter gave testimony of her tender care, *"the comfort of her hand,"* her *"gentle"* touch in giving back rubs and baths, and the ease with which she turned bodies.

Yet missionaries and local Christians were not her only social circles. Halima had links with the small Ethiopian community in Cairo, through whom she learned definitively of her parents' deaths. Perhaps she had kept alive a hope of returning home to them one day. In 1928, at about the age of fifty-two, she retired from work at the hospital and married a younger Ethiopian man living in Cairo, finally settling down. The missionary community feared the younger man was after her money and initially begrudged her the companionship and intimacy that marriage might bring. Having worked for half a century and lived in other peoples' homes, she established her own home and balcony garden. At the same time, she rekindled ties with some of her "sisters," the freed slaves from boarding school days. When one was widowed and unable to care for her daughter, Halima took the girl in and raised her as her own. *"The joy and pride of motherhood became hers in this girl,"* her pamphleteer wrote. The girl later became the wife of the Ethiopian ambassador to the USA. With a "daughter" to support, Halima went back to work as a nurse, caring for the mother of one of the missionaries. In her leisure in the invalid's home, she read from her Arabic Bible and the *Women's Missionary Magazine*. But the nurse was losing strength and was sent to Tanta Hospital for testing. There she was diagnosed with terminal cancer and died in August 1934 at about the age of fifty-eight in the hospital where she had served for decades.

Her pamphleteer concluded, *"It had been no small responsibility to take into a little school family a dozen of wild orphans of another race and color.*

Infinite patience and Christian love were lavished on the child Halima. How gloriously she repaid the sacrifice." Her devotion, service, and *"victorious testimony in the hour of death"* reaffirmed the missionaries' decision to take in the freed slave girls sent by Baring. Of all the freed African slave girls, Halima's life most closely followed the missionaries' script for a life of service, at least in their telling. Halima's perspective remains elusive.

References

1 A. A. Brown, "Susan Ameen," Cairo, Nov. 1891 in *Women's Missionary Magazine* 5, no.6 (Jan. 1892), 166-67.

2 Anna Y. Thompson, "Mission Work in Egypt," *Women's Missionary Magazine* 5, no.3 (Oct. 1891), 68.

3 *Anti-Slavery Reporter* (March-April 1893), (Jan. 1885), 259; (Aug. 1885), 449-50; (May-June 1886), 57-58;

4 Beth Baron, *Egypt as a Woman: Nationalism, Gender, and Politics* (Berkeley: University of California Press, 2005), chap.1;

5 C.C. Scott Moncrieff, "The Treasurer's Report-1886," *Anti-Slavery Reporter* (May-June 1886), 58; Crewe, "Slave Trade in Egypt," 61, (Oct. 6 - Dec. 1885), 595.

6 Charles C. Starbuck, "Theological

and Religious Intelligence," *The Andover Review* (May 1889), 529.

7 Diane Robinson-Dunne, *The Harem, Slavery and British Imperial Culture: Anglo-Muslim Relations in the Late Nineteenth Century* (Manchester: Manchester University Press, 2006), 84-92.

8 Du Port, "Report" 69;

9 E. Crewe, "The Slave Trade in Egypt," Cairo, April 9, 1886 in *Anti-Slavery Re- porter* (May-June 1886), 61.

10 Ehud R. Toledano, *As If Silent and Absent: Bonds of Enslavement in the Islamic Middle East* (New Haven: Yale University Press, 2007);

11 Eve M. Troutt Powell, A Different Shade of Colonialism: Egypt, Great

Britain, and the Mastery of the Sudan (Berkeley: University of California Press, 2003).

12 Gabriel Baer, "Slavery in Nineteenth Century Egypt," *Journal of African History* 8, no.3 (1967): 417-41; reprinted as "Slavery and Its Abolition," in *Studies in the Social History of Modern Egypt* (Chicago: University of Chicago Press, 1969), chap.10.

13 George M. La Rue, "The Capture of a Slave Caravan: The Incident at Asyut (Egypt) in 1880," *African Economic History*, No.30 (2002), 89.

14 *Halima*, 3-4, 7; "Egypt," *Anti-Slavery Reporter* (March-April 1893), 63.

15 *Halima—The Gentle One* (Pittsburgh: Women's General Missionary Society,

United Presbyterian Church of North American, n.d.), 7.

16 Hilal, "The Anti-Slavery Movement in Egypt in the Nineteenth Century: Between Shari`a and Practice" (paper presented at a workshop on "Race and Slavery Between the Middle East and Africa," CUNY Graduate Center, 23 April 2004).

17 Imad Hilal, *al-Raqiq fi Misr fi al-qarn al-tisa' `ashar* (Cairo: al-`Arabi, 1999).

18 John Hunwick and Eve Troutt Powell, *The African Diaspora in the Mediterranean Lands of Islam* (Princeton: Markus Wiener Publishers, 2002.

19 John Hunwick, "The Religious Practices of Black Slaves in the

Mediterranean Islamic World," in *Slavery on the Frontiers of Islam,* ed. Paul E. Lovejoy (Princeton: Markus Wiener Publishers, 2004), 149-171.

20 Judith E. Tucker, *Women in Nineteenth-Century Egypt* (Cambridge: Cambridge University Press, 1985), 191-92.

21 Kozma, "Women at the Margins," chap.3.

22 Liat Kozma, "Women on the Margins and Legal Reform in Late Nineteenth- Century Egypt, 1850-1882" (Ph.D. dissertation, New York University, 2006).

23 M. S. P. Du Port, "Report of the Cairo Committee for the Year 1886," in *Anti- Slavery Reporter* (March-

April 1887), 69.

24 Mary L. Whately, *Letters from Egypt to Plain Folks at Home* (London: Seeley, Jackson, & Halliday, 1879), 240-257

25 Mowafi, *Slavery,* 37.

26 Muhafazat Asyut, *Asyut fi 10 Sanawat* (Cairo: Matba`at Nahdat Misr, 1962.

27 Presbyterian Historical Society (PHS), Anna Thompson Papers, RG 58, box 1, folder 4, Notebook: Red Letter Days, 57, 59. The event is noted as occurring on March 1 and March 7.

28 Reda Mowafi, *Slavery, Slave Trade, and Abolition Attempts in Egypt and the Sudan, 1820-1882* (Stockholm: Esselte Studium, 1981).

29 Rhodes House Library, British and Foreign Anti-Slavery Society, S22, G25, Africa, No. 4 (1887), Correspondence Respecting Slavery in Egypt, Enclosure 2 in No.1, Lieutenant-Colonel Schaefer to Captain Crawford, Commandant, Suez, 25 Oct. 1886, 4.

30 Sara Pursley, "From Civil War to Civilizing Mission: American Military Officers in the Egyptian Service, 1869-1879" (paper presented at a workshop on "Race and Slavery between the Middle East and Africa," CUNY Graduate Center, 23 April 2004).

31 Toledano, *Silent and Absent*, chap.3.

32 Toledano, *Slavery and Abolition in the Ottoman Middle East* (Seattle: University of Washington Press 1998.

33 Y. Hakan Erdem, *Slavery in the Ottoman Empire and Its Demise, 1800-1909* (New York: St. Martin's Press, 1996).

34 Ahmed Hussein. Benevolent masters and voiceless subjects: slavery and slave trade in southern Wällo (Ethiopia) in the 19th and early 20th centuries. In: Annales d'Ethiopie. Volume 25, année 2010. pp. 197-208;